SCHOOL PEOPLE

Poems selected by **LEE BENNETT HOPKINS**

Illustrated by **ELLEN SHI**

WORD∫ONG

An Imprint of Highlights
HONESDALE, PENNSYLVANIA

To the Lowman family–
Caleb, Tara, Alexa, Chloe, and Aaron–who open so many doors.
—LBH

To my kindergarten teacher,
Dr. Moretti, my first and favorite teacher
—ES

ACKNOWLEDGMENTS

Thanks are due to the following for use of works in this collection:

Curtis Brown, Ltd. for "School's Story" and "School's Story Reprise" by Rebecca Kai Dotlich, copyright © 2018 by Rebecca Kai Dotlich; "Librarian" by Lee Bennett Hopkins, copyright © 2018 by Lee Bennett Hopkins; "Nurse" by Amy Ludwig VanDerwater, copyright © 2018 by Amy Ludwig VanDerwater. All printed by permission of Curtis Brown, Ltd.

All other works are used by permission of the respective poets who control all rights: Alma Flor Ada for "Spanish Teacher"; Robyn Hood Black for "Lunch Lady"; Matt Forrest Esenwine for "Bus Driver"; Charles Ghigna for "Coach"; Joan Bransfield Graham for "Teacher"; Michele Krueger for "Art Teacher"; Renée M. LaTulippe for "Theater Teacher"; Irene Latham for "Music Teacher"; J. Patrick Lewis for "Principal"; Ann Whitford Paul for "Crossing Guard"; Darren Sardelli for "Custodian."

Special thanks to Rebecca M. Davis, a forever-teacher.

WordSong
An Imprint of Highlights
815 Church Street
Honesdale, Pennsylvania 18431
Printed in China

ISBN: 978-1-62979-703-8

Library of Congress Control Number: 2017942353
First edition

Designed by Katie Jennings Campbell
The text of this book is set in Argone and Might Could Sans.
The artwork is done digitally.

10 9 8 7 6 5 4 3 2 1

CONTENTS

SCHOOL'S STORY

REBECCA KAI DOTLICH

I am waiting—come on in!

Welcome to this house of brick.
Enter whispers, whistles, signs,
footsteps, fossils, notebook lines.

Rooms hold calendars, chairs, and nooks,
murals, maps, library books.
Feet scamper, shuffle, dash, drum.
Listen to my hallway hum!

I am waiting—come on in!

Hear a chorus of rings and knocks,
a clatter of ladders, letters, rocks.
The swishing of brooms, the clicking of locks.

In my house are all these parts:
markers, makers, ceiling art.
A building full of soul and heart.

Clocks tick and tock,
        tock and tick—
in and around this house of brick.

I am waiting—come on in!

4

5

BUS DRIVER

MATT FORREST ESENWINE

Your good-morning smile
waits behind
a folding double door;
another day
to work and play,
to laugh, to learn—explore.

Time goes by so quickly;
the last bell rings,
and then—
that smiling face
I know so well
will bring me home again.

CROSSING GUARD

ANN WHITFORD PAUL

We wait by the curb
while she,
wearing her bright orange vest,
arms wide like wings,
swoops into the street.

"*Tweet, tweet,*" her whistle sings.
Cars grumble to a stop.
She beckons us to walk,
hovers close,
guides us
like hatchlings
safely
to the other side—

our crossing-guard bird.

PRINCIPAL

J. PATRICK LEWIS

Who could ever guess
that my School Principal
would wipe tears from the face
of a first-grader,

find the milk snake
that escaped from the Science Room,

grow a vast vegetable garden
in the school courtyard,

teach a bully
how to be humble,

and also be the Principal of me?

See you after school, Mom!

TEACHER

JOAN BRANSFIELD GRAHAM

9

You have so many talents.
    You do everything with flair.
Any minute I'm expecting...
    you will rise up in the air.

You stretch my world much wider.
    Your stories lift me high.
They spark imagination—

    I feel I, too, can fly.

SPANISH TEACHER

ALMA FLOR ADA

We are learning Spanish,
savoring
new sounds.

Mom is *mamá*.
Dad is *papá*.

Rose is *rosa*.
Butterfly, *mariposa*.

Cat is *gato*.
Duck, *pato*.

Lion is *león*.
Champion, *campeón*.

Boy is *niño*.
Love, *cariño*.

As we learn Spanish,
we spice up
a world
twice as flavorful.

LUNCH LADY

ROBYN HOOD BLACK

Long before lunchtime
Ms. Bailey keeps busy
stacking towers of trays,
filling the salad bar,
sliding steaming pans
into place.

We swarm the cafeteria.
"Here you go, Honey," she says,
handing each of us a full plate.

Long after lunchtime
Ms. Bailey scrubs everything clean,
hangs the last heavy pan.

She rubs her neck,
wipes her forehead,
and changes the menu sign
for us—
for tomorrow.

CUSTODIAN

DARREN SARDELLI

He holds the keys to every door,
clears and mops the lunchroom floor,
empties trash cans, sweeps the stairs,
fixes tables, desks, and chairs.

He makes each sink and fountain shine.
He's caring, helpful, smart, and kind.
He keeps our building neat and clean,
yet—this man is rarely seen!

ART TEACHER

MICHELE KRUEGER

In her room
a brown lump of clay
becomes a triceratops I ride across a prehistoric plain.

In her room
green crayons grow a jungle
where monkeys swing from branches
in a tropical rain.

In her room
a white sheet of paper
flies me past the Milky Way
in the folds of an origami crane.

In her room
my mind wanders
my imagination soars.

There is no time or place
on Earth or in space
I can't explore.

In her room
I am an artist.

MUSIC TEACHER

IRENE LATHAM

She walks in music, like morning rain:

drip-drop, pitter-patter, boot-stomp, splash!

And all that's best of noise and silence
meet in her flash-flood smile.

She doesn't say *Hush* or *Stop* or *No*—
she says, *Yes! Louder! Sing, my angels, sing!*

And so our hearts overflow;
symphonies river from our lips.

We walk in music like morning rain:

drip-drop, pitter-patter, boot-stomp, splash!

COACH

CHARLES GHIGNA

A whistle
a shout
a helping hand

a smile
applause
my biggest fan

24

a stretch
a race
a new game to play

Coach is the one
leading the way

steering
cheering
teaching us all

life is a gym
come—
have a ball

THEATER TEACHER

RENÉE LATULIPPE

With him we adventure,
examine, explore.
We sail out to sea,
we drift back to shore.

We toddle like turtles,
we *SHUSH!* in our shells.
Our teacher is always
casting his spells…

*Za-ZING! You're a daisy!
Reach high to the sky!*

Our hands hover over
our heads—petals fly!

Wa-WHOOP! You're a wolf!
Now sing a wolf tune!

We prowl and howl
a-WOOO! at the moon.

Pa-POW! You're a cowboy,
a pirate, a spy.

We wrangle, we *AARGH!*
We're mysterious, sly.

With him we are anything
we want to be.
We saunter like lions.
We're fearless.

We're *free!*

LIBRARIAN

LEE BENNETT HOPKINS

He opened the door.

As we walked in
he said,

"Look!
It's all about books.
And books are you!

Books will lead you
anywhere
everywhere—
to magical places
to meet new faces."

He opened
one single door
yet he
led us down
pathways
we never
could ever
have traveled
before.

NURSE

AMY LUDWIG VANDERWATER

Every day
a new parade
of sniffles and scratches
marches through
her open door.

She looks at us,
listens,
heals our hurts
big and small.

Even when I'm well
it helps to know
she's here
like the heart in my body
like the moon in our sky.

SCHOOL'S STORY REPRISE

REBECCA KAI DOTLICH

In my house are all these parts;
hours of wonders, surprises, starts.

Clocks tick and tock,
tock and tick—

in and around my house of brick.